CONTENTS

THE BENIN KINGDOM

Where and when?

The Benin Kingdom was founded in around CE 900. At this time, the Edo people of West Africa began settling in the rainforests of what is now southern Nigeria. At first they lived in many separate villages. Over time, these communities grew and flourished to form a strong, united kingdom that the Edo called Igodomigodo.

The early Edo people were ruled by men called Ogisos, which means 'sky-kings'. This period of Ogiso rule is known as the first dynasty. The Ogisos lost power in around 1180 and, after a brief period without any kings at all, the second dynasty began. The new rulers were known as Obas.

This map shows the Benin Kingdom and the surrounding kingdoms.

River Niger

River Niger

Dahomey Kingdom

Yoruba Kingdom

Asante Kingdom

Ife

Cameroon Grasslands Kingdom

Atlantic Ocean

Benin City

Benin Kingdom

Benin at its height

Under the Obas, Benin became a wealthy, successful empire, centred on its great capital, Benin City. The Edo people enjoyed successful trading relationships with other African kingdoms and, later, with several European countries. For 200 years, a series of strong warrior kings kept their citizens safe and protected the kingdom from attack by neighbouring peoples.

What happened?

In the 1600s, after a succession of weak Obas, the kingdom began to decline. By the 1800s, Benin was no longer the great empire it had once been. This made it an easy target for greedy outsiders. The British wanted access to the resources that Benin had to offer, including rubber and palm oil. In 1897, they invaded the Benin Kingdom and Benin City was burned to the ground. Afterwards, Benin became part of the British Empire.

The people of Benin became famous for their works of art. Plaques such as this one of a drummer, from the Oba's palace, are known as the 'Benin Bronzes', although they are actually made of brass.

When a group of British officials entered Benin after they had been told to leave, they were killed. This event triggered the invasion that ended the Kingdom of Benin.

WARRIOR KINGS

The Benin Kingdom's greatest asset was its strong leaders, or Obas. Under a series of five great warrior kings, the empire grew to its greatest extent and power.

From Ogiso to Oba

The Ogisos ruled the early Benin Kingdom until the 1100s. Then, the Ogisos grew weak and began to lose control of the kingdom. The leaders of different villages began to fight one another. To help restore peace, the Edo people asked a prince from Ife, in the nearby Yoruba Kingdom, to help. The prince's son, Eweka, established the second dynasty in the Benin Kingdom — the rule of the Obas.

This painting from the 1600s shows an Oba on his horse in a procession. The king played an important part in Edo rituals and celebrations.

Ewuare the Great

The first of the five great warrior Obas, Ewuare, came to the throne in around 1440. During his 40-year reign, Benin became a strong, powerful kingdom. Ewuare began trading with Portuguese merchants (see page 19), which made the kingdom wealthy and enabled the Oba to pay for a large army. In turn, the army conquered new territory and expanded the kingdom.

Building the Edo empire

Ewuare's son, Ozolua, was a great soldier, who won many battles and extended the kingdom even further. The next Oba, Esigie, was responsible for expanding the kingdom eastwards, including conquering parts of the Yoruba Kingdom.

The empire reached its greatest extent under Oba Orhogbua. By the end of his reign, Benin stretched beyond the River Niger and westwards to what is now Ghana. The fifth great warrior king was Ehengbuda. Despite threats by rebellious local chieftains, he was strong enough to keep control of the empire. After his death in about 1601, however, the Benin Kingdom began to decline.

This brass plaque, from the Oba's palace, is believed to depict the warrior king Ozolua.

The Edo believed that an ancient king of Benin wrestled the god Olokun and won, earning the right to wear coral.

TEST OF TIME

Although the British conquered Benin in 1897, the Obas remained the spiritual leaders of the Edo people. There are still Obas in Nigeria today, and they play an important part in Edo culture and traditions.

THE POWER OF THE OBA

The Oba had control over almost every aspect of the Benin Kingdom. He owned all the land, and decided what it should be used for.

A life of luxury

The Oba resided in a grand palace complex in the heart of Benin City. Hundreds of people lived at this court, making sure the Oba had everything he wanted. The Oba had several wives and lots of children, so many staff were needed to take care of him and his family.

WOW!

The Oba's mother, known as Iyoba, or queen mother, was also an important figure in Edo society. She was said to have special powers. She was not allowed to see her son after he became Oba in case she tried to use magic to control him!

This ivory pendant shows an Iyoba (mother of the Oba). It may be Idia, wife of Oba Ozolua and mother of Oba Esigie.

Honouring the Oba

The Oba was regarded as a god, and was respected and revered by his subjects. In the presence of the Oba, ordinary people had to remain kneeling. They were not allowed to look directly at him. The Oba himself was thought to have magic powers, and special festivals were held every year to renew these powers.

Keeping control

The first Oba, Ewuare, established a system of town chiefs, who could report on what happened in the provinces of Benin. As time passed, the Oba employed even more advisors so he would know what was happening all across his kingdom. The Uzama, or elders, were the most important. Other advisors came from villages outside the city. They had many different jobs, such as farmers, soldiers or craftworkers, so they could advise the Oba on different things.

Benin art often showed animals that represented the Oba's powers. These two ivory leopards were placed on either side of his throne during ceremonies.

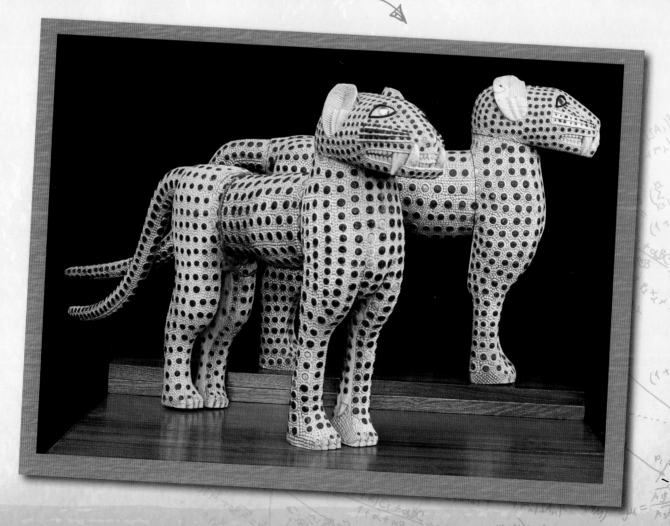

SOCIAL STRUCTURE

There was a strict structure to society in the Benin Kingdom. The Oba was at the top, of course. Below him were the members of his family and the nobles. They were wealthier than the ordinary people, but everyone had what they needed – the Benin people were comfortable and happy.

Forgive and forget

In Benin City, there were captains who acted as judges when people disagreed with one another. The justice system was based on forgiveness. If someone was found guilty of stealing, they could apologise and return or replace the goods. If they did so, they would not be punished. When Europeans first arrived in Benin City, they were amazed at how little crime there was!

This picture shows a scene of daily life in Benin City, with the Oba's palace at the heart of the city.

Daily life

The Europeans were surprised at how happy ordinary people seemed to be. There were no beggars — no one was homeless or hungry. The streets were wide and clean, and the houses were large and well-maintained. Every house had its own well to provide the family with fresh water. Visitors reported that Benin City was so free from crime that many of the houses had doorways but no doors!

The slave trade

Not everyone in Benin had such a contented life, though. Traders in Benin both bought and sold slaves. These slaves were usually taken from lands conquered by the Edo, then sold to other parts of Africa. However, some remained in Benin City to work for noblemen who lived there. To begin with, slaves were mostly women, but by around 1700, men were also being bought and sold. In general, people treated their slaves well, and allowed them to earn their freedom.

TEST of TIME

The Edo left no written records so it is difficult to know what life was really like for ordinary people. What we know about the Benin Kingdom today comes from reports by Europeans who visited Benin City, and from the art of the Edo people that survives today.

Europeans would bid for slaves at slave markets in Africa.

RELIGION

The people of Benin worshipped many gods and goddesses. The festivals held to honour them were an important part of life in the kingdom.

GENIUS ★ IMPORTANT BELIEFS

Gods of the Edo people

Osanobua is the creator god in the Edo religion — the god who is believed to have made the world. The word 'Osanobua' means 'god' in the Edo language. Osanobua's children became the main gods worshipped by the Edo people. His son, Olokun, was ruler of the oceans. He was also thought to bring wealth and fertility to the land.

Osanobua's daughter, Obiemven, was the goddess of childbirth and farming. Another of Osanobua's sons, Ogiuwu, was the god of death.

This plaque shows two men performing a ritual at a festival. They are using ropes in a special dance to honour the god of war and iron, Ogun.

WOW!

Religion in the Benin Kingdom involved one gruesome practice — human sacrifice. When an Oba died, it was considered an honour for his closest friends and ministers to be killed and buried with their leader.

The spirit world

The Edo people believed that the universe was divided into two regions — the everyday world and the spirit world. The gods and ancestors lived in the spirit world, but they could affect the lives of people in the everyday world. The Edo also thought that powerful humans, such as witch doctors, could talk to the gods and use their power to heal the sick.

Celebrating festivals

Religious festivals were held throughout the year to honour the gods and the Oba. Festivals also marked important seasonal events, such as harvest time. Everyone contributed to the festival in some way, whether by growing food for the feasts or by making costumes for the parades and celebrations.

TEST OF TIME

Some traditional ceremonies to honour the gods are still held by the Edo people today, such as the festival of Igue, which takes place at the end of each year. The festival is believed to bring good luck to the Oba and his people.

The Oba always attended festivals in Benin City. In this picture, the Oba (on the horse) is leading a procession of musicians from his palace during a festival.

PROFESSIONAL SOLDIERS

GENIUS
★ WELL-TRAINED ARMY ★

To build and control his empire, the Oba needed a strong, disciplined fighting force. Ozolua and Esigie, in particular (see page 7), established huge armies – and put them to use!

The commander-in-chief

The Oba was the head of the army. He had his own royal regiment, and these hand-picked men served as his personal bodyguards as well as soldiers. The Oba decided when the kingdom should go to war, and he worked with military commanders to plan conquests. Some Obas even led their armies into battle.

This statue from the Benin Kingdom shows a warrior on horseback.

14

Structure of the army

The Benin army was very well organised. The Oba relied on a network of commanders including the Iyase, the commander of the army regiments in the city. However, men from all over the kingdom served in the army. Groups from villages beyond the city walls formed the backbone of the fighting force. They answered immediately when the Oba called them to arms. They carried hand-made shields crafted from wood and animal skins.

Weapons of war

At first, most soldiers fought with swords and spears made of brass and iron, and with wooden crossbows. In the 1400s, Portuguese traders arrived in Benin with weapons the Edo had never seen before — guns. Because the Benin people were not Christians, the Portuguese refused to sell them guns. However, some Portuguese joined the Benin army as paid soldiers and used guns against the Edo's enemies. It was not until the 1690s that Dutch traders started selling guns to Benin.

This plaque from the Oba's palace shows a Portuguese soldier with a gun called a matchlock.

WOW!

Oba Ozolua was a legendary soldier. It is said that he won around 200 battles — a record that earned him the nickname 'Ozolua the Conqueror'.

DESIGN AND ENGINEERING

In the days before construction machinery and computers, the people of the Benin Kingdom proved themselves geniuses at town planning and engineering. The construction of Benin City was one of their greatest achievements.

Original Benin City

There were small villages scattered all across the Benin Kingdom, but most of the population was concentrated in Benin City. The city was burned to the ground when the British invaded in 1897, and almost nothing remains of it today. Most of what we know comes from written accounts by Europeans who visited Benin from the 1400s onwards.

A grand plan

These visitors seem to have been impressed by Benin City. They said it was grand and clean, with lots of space. They remarked on how well it was planned and designed. Its smart clay houses lined long, straight streets. Benin City was also one of the first cities to have street lights. These were large metal lamps that were lit at night using palm oil.

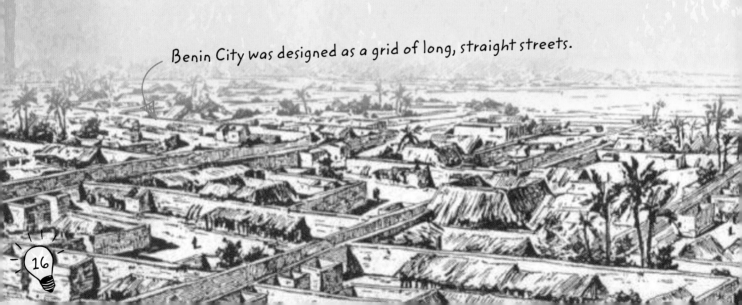

Benin City was designed as a grid of long, straight streets.

City defences

To keep the capital city safe from attack, it was surrounded by deep ditches in the north and huge walls in the south. The walls of Benin City were an engineering marvel.

Built between CE 800 and 1500, they covered more than 1,000 km. They were the largest earthwork structure in the world. Although none of the city walls remain, experts think that at one time they may have been four times as long as the Great Wall of China.

(((BRAIN WAVE)))

As well as the city walls, there were hundreds of other walls that divided the outskirts of the city into around 500 separate but connected settlements. This created one huge, united kingdom.

WOW!

The outer settlement walls were built by ordinary men and women, not construction workers. It is estimated that it took 150 million hours of digging to lay the foundations for the walls.

Only a few of the ancient earthworks and ditches that surrounded the old city can still be seen.

ditch

earthwork

TRADE

Trade was essential to the success of the Benin Kingdom, bringing wealth and power to the Oba and his people. Trading was considered an important profession.

GENIUS ★ THRIVING ECONOMY

Neighbourly trade

As the Benin Kingdom grew under the rule of the Obas, the Benin people came into contact with other African peoples and began trading with them. The River Niger (see map on page 4) to the north of Benin City provided a perfect trade route. Goods could be easily transported to nearby African kingdoms along the river.

(see map on page 4)

(((BRAIN WAVE)))

The Edo people wanted to show their strength against cheats and thieves. If a foreign trader stole from a Benin trader, no one from Benin would trade with anyone from the same region or country as the thieving trader until they had apologised and returned the goods.

Portuguese traders like the ones shown on this plaque were the first to arrive. They must have looked strange to the people of Benin.

Overseas traders

Later, the Atlantic Ocean to the south opened up the kingdom to trade with European countries. The first Portuguese merchant ships arrived in 1485 and, later, the Dutch, British, French and Spanish all came to trade with the Benin Kingdom. These foreign merchants were not allowed in Benin villages. Instead, they would meet at an agreed location and would carry out their trade there. Sometimes negotiations between the two sides would last for weeks!

Goods for sale

Trade in Africa did not involve money. Instead, people traded goods for other things that they wanted. The people of Benin valued foreign items such as brass bracelets from Europe, which they could melt down and use in their own metalworking (see page 26). They also bought luxury items such as coral and cloth. In exchange, Benin traders offered goods including ivory from elephant tusks and food such as peppercorns, which were very popular in Europe.

This carved ivory salt cellar from the 1600s depicts European traders and their ship.

WOW!

Cowrie shells were a highly prized item in the Benin Kingdom. They were used as a form of money, and each Oba would display his collection of shells as a show of wealth.

European traders often arrived loaded with cowrie shells to trade with the Benin people.

FARMING

Crops were important to the Benin Kingdom. They were not just used to feed the population – they were also valuable trade goods. Farming was another respected profession among the Edo people.

Crops and livestock

Farmers lived in villages outside Benin City. They cleared nearby areas of rainforest to grow crops. The main crop was yams, but farmers also grew beans, rice, peanuts, millet, sorghum, onions and cotton. They grew pepper too, which was much sought-after by European traders. Villagers raised livestock such as sheep, goats and cattle for food.

This plaque shows a servant collecting fruit. Mango, papaya and other tropical fruits were common in the Benin Kingdom.

Yams, a type of sweet potato, were the staple crop in the Benin Kingdom. Ordinary people probably ate them at every meal. Yams are still a staple of the local diet today.

Division of labour

The people in a village all shared responsibility for the surrounding farmland. In farming villages, men sowed, tended and harvested the main crops such as yams. The men worked together with friends and relatives to make sure there was a good harvest. Women were in charge of the less important crops such as onions, which were grown in smaller areas. Women were also responsible for selling farm produce in the markets.

Hunting and fishing

Wild animals, such as deer and antelope, lived in the rainforests. The men would hunt these with bows and arrows, then cook them for meat. Larger animals, such as elephants and leopards, also lived in the forests. But only a few men were given permission by the Oba to hunt them for their ivory and skins.

This ivory figure from the 1600s shows a woman from the Benin Kingdom kneeling, carrying a bowl on her head.

TEST OF TIME

In ancient times, the Oba owned all the land and could decide how it was allocated. The ruler of the Edo people still officially owns the land in this part of Nigeria, centred on Benin City, although today this is a more symbolic ownership.

THE ART OF BENIN

The Benin Kingdom is best known for its amazing art. Artists and craftworkers were skilled in all different types of art. They worked in many different materials, from clay and wood to precious metal and ivory.

Masks of the gods

Carved wooden masks from the Benin Kingdom show amazing skill and artistry. They were often made for special ceremonies to honour the Oba. Because of this, many masks took the shape of animals such as leopards, which represented the king. The crocodile was also an important animal in Benin culture, representing the Oba's swift justice against those who opposed him.

Coral and ivory

Coral was believed to be a gift from the sea god Olokun, so it was very valuable in Benin culture. Craftworkers made beautiful jewellery from coral, such as necklaces and bracelets. Ivory was also a precious material. Because it came from elephant tusks, it was a symbol of strength and purity. Only the Oba and a few important chiefs were allowed to wear jewellery that had been carved from ivory.

Leopards were considered the king of animals, so they were a common symbol of the Oba's power in Benin art.

Village crafts

In the villages outside Benin City, craftworkers created practical items such as clay pots and bowls. There were also blacksmiths who made tools and weapons for others in their village. They wove cloth out of cotton fibres. These were often created in colourful striped patterns, using dye made from plant extracts. Fabric like this was traded with people from other African kingdoms and tribes.

cotton plant

WOW!

The Edo people may have invented the African instrument called the thumb piano, or mbira. This is a small wooden board fitted with metal 'fingers' that play different notes when they are plucked.

thumb piano

Some traditional pieces are still used today. This carved ivory tusk is being used in a ceremony to mark the coronation of the new Oba.

CRAFT GUILDS

A guild is a group of artists or craftworkers who practise the same trade. In the Benin Kingdom, members of a guild lived and worked together, and supported each other to protect their joint interests.

Ere's idea

The guild system was established in the Benin Kingdom during the rule of the Ogisos. Ogiso Ere came to the throne in about CE 16 and ruled for 60 years. During that time, trade with neighbouring tribes increased and there was a great demand for arts and crafts. Ere decided to organise his workers into guilds, believing that this would guarantee the highest standards. He wanted Benin art to be better than anywhere else's.

This brass bracelet depicts faces and mudfish. The mudfish was considered a special creature because it can breathe on land and underwater.

Guilds for everything

At the height of the kingdom, under the great warrior Obas, there were more than forty guilds in Benin City. There were guilds for wood carvers, ivory carvers, leather workers, blacksmiths, weavers, and many other artists and craftworkers. Each guild had a special job to perform for the Oba. The most famous and important guild was the brass-casters' guild (see pages 26–27).

(see pages 26–27).

WOW!

It was not only craftworkers who belonged to guilds in ancient Benin society. There were also guilds for doctors, leopard hunters, acrobats and dancers — all professions that the Oba valued.

Grand designs

Within the guilds, the craftworkers competed to make the most beautiful and eye-catching pieces they could. They would come up with their own designs intended to please the Oba. They believed that these designs were inspired by the gods and the spirits of their ancestors.

'Altars to the hand' such as this were special sculptures created to honour particular individuals. This one honours Ehenua, an Ezomo, or military commander.

TEST OF TIME

There are still craftworkers' guilds in Benin City today. They continue to make beautiful objects for the Oba, but now they also make them to sell to locals and visitors alike.

BENIN BRASS

From the time of Ogiso rule, from around CE 900, the Benin people produced amazing metalwork. The Oba's palace was filled with beautiful brass plaques, masks and statues.

The brass-casters' guild

Brass is an alloy of the metals copper and zinc. It can be used to make practical objects, such as plates and bowls, but it can also be shaped into works of art. Brass-casters were the most highly skilled and greatly admired workers in the Benin Kingdom. They were so important that they were only allowed to work for the Oba, and everything they made belonged to him.

Brass-casters still work in Benin City today, creating art in the way the Edo have done for centuries.

The power of brass

People believed that brass had magical powers and could ward off evil. Because of this, the Oba surrounded himself with brass objects. These pieces depicted Obas and other important people, as well as scenes from famous battles and other historical events. When the British invaded, they took more than a thousand of these 'Benin Bronzes' from the palace. Many can still be seen in the British Museum in London.

Casting brass

Craftworkers used a process called 'lost-wax casting' to make these beautiful artworks. First, they created a model of the piece out of wax. This was buried in sand and then heated so that the wax melted into the sand, leaving a hollow, shaped mould. The brass was made by melting down copper and mixing it with molten tin. The liquid was poured into the mould and left to cool. Then the mould was broken open to reveal the piece, which was polished to a high shine — ready to present to the Oba.

WOW!

For religious reasons, women were not allowed to be metal-workers — in fact, they were not allowed to touch metal at all. Women were only allowed to be members of the weavers' guild.

This brass head was made using the 'lost-wax' method. It may represent the sea god, Olokun.

MEDICINE

GENIUS ★ HERBAL CURES ★

Medicine in the Benin Kingdom was a mixture of religion and herbalism. The Edo put their faith in witch doctors and people who knew about herbs.

The wrath of the gods

People in ancient Benin believed that illness could be caused by the anger of the gods or ancestors. If someone committed a crime, they might risk the wrath of the gods. And if people did not honour their ancestors in the right way, it was believed that these spirits might take revenge by inflicting a serious illness on them.

Diseases from overseas

When European traders first arrived in Benin, they brought with them diseases such as smallpox. The Edo had never been exposed to foreign diseases like this before. They did not know what they were and had no idea how to treat them. They thought that this must be a punishment from the gods.

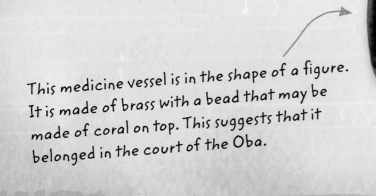

This medicine vessel is in the shape of a figure. It is made of brass with a bead that may be made of coral on top. This suggests that it belonged in the court of the Oba.

Natural medicines

The people of ancient Benin knew that some plants could ease certain ailments. The rainforests they lived in had many healing plants. The Edo grew some herbs for use in cooking and to help heal wounds. The god of medicine and healing was Osun, and the Edo also referred to 'osun' as the power contained in plants and herbs to heal and cure.

(((BRAIN WAVE)))

As they had no way of writing things down, Edo elders passed on knowledge orally. Every evening, villagers would gather round a campfire and listen to storytellers weaving tales. They told of the history of the Edo people, the founding of the Benin Kingdom, myths and legends about the gods, as well as passing on knowledge of herbal cures and other practical things.

This hip pendant would have been worn during rituals to honour the god Osun, linking the Oba with the 'magic' power of herbs and leaves.

GLOSSARY

alloy — a mixture of two metals

ancestor — someone from a family who lived a long time ago

coral — a hard pink material made from a sea animal

dynasty — a line of rulers who inherited the throne from one another

guild — an organisation of people who have the same job

herbalism — the use of herbs to treat illnesses

ivory — a hard material from the tusks of an elephant

Iyoba — the mother of the Oba

Oba — a king of the Edo people

Ogiso — a ruler of the Edo people during the first dynasty

palm oil — oil from palm trees that is used for cooking and making things such as soap and candles

plaque — a flat piece of metal or stone that has writing or images on it

ritual — a religious ceremony where certain actions are carried out

sacrifice — when an animal (or person) is killed to make the gods happy

witch doctor — a member of a tribe who is believed to have powers of healing and communicating with gods and ancestors

TIMELINE

CE 16   Ogiso Ere becomes ruler of Benin and establishes the guild system.

CE 900s   Edo people settle in the rainforests of West Africa.

1180   Ogisos lose power, leading to about twenty years with no ruler, followed by the second dynasty of the Obas.

1440   Ewuare becomes Oba – the first of the five great warrior kings.

1450   Work is completed on the walls of Benin City.

1485   Portuguese traders arrive in Benin.

1601   Ehengbuda dies – the last of the great warrior Obas.

1690s   Dutch traders start selling guns to the Edo people.

1700   Men start being sold as slaves as well as women.

1897   The British invade Benin and make it a colony of Britain.

INDEX

FURTHER INFORMATION

Websites

www.bbc.co.uk/guides/z3s2xnb

www.britishmuseum.org/pdf/KingdomOfBenin_Presentation.pdf

www.ks2history.com/benin-guide

Books

Benin (Explore!) by Izzi Howell (Wayland, 2019)

Benin Empire (Great Civilisations) by Catherine Chambers (Franklin Watts, 2016)